Effective Business Communications

These Must Be Some of the Best Kept Communications Secrets in the World!

By Sasha Diaz

© 2014 All Rights Reserved

Text copyright reserved. Sasha Diaz

The contents of this book may not be reproduced, duplicated or transmitted without direct written permission from the author.

ISBN-13: 978-1505686821
ISBN-10: 1505686822

Disclaimer: All attempts have been made by the author to provide factual and accurate content. No responsibility will be taken by the author or publisher for any damages caused by misuse of the contents described in this book. The content of this book has been derived from various sources. Please consult an expert before attempting anything described in this book.

CONTENTS

	Introduction	i
1	Dissecting Modern day business communication	1
2	Developing your listening skills	12
3	Non verbal communication skills	18
4	Cultural Considerations in Business Communication	23
5	Qualities of a Good Business Communication	26
6	On Business Writing	34
	Conclusion	

Introduction

Why is there a need to communicate?
Let's use this analogy: The parts of a computer may not seem to talk or at least have never heard or observe them talk. These parts, however, work in such a mathematically precise way that a task is began as soon as another is finished or that a task is never performed while another task which could be in conflict with the present task is finished. This very precision and coordination is what makes a computer, a man-made machine, so efficient and useful.

Yet how do they do it? It's simple: each part communicates with other parts.

Their means of communication may be uniquely and purely machine-based, yet without this, it may never work.
The same is true with a business. A business is not a solitary entity. Its success is greatly dependent upon the number of connections is create. These connections will help a business run its many operations smoothly and help it earn and profit from those.

Three types of connections are involved in business: 1. between the persons inside the business which is important for its smooth functioning, 2. between the business and other businesses, and 3. between the business and the clients.

Chapter I. Dissecting Modern-Day Business Communication

Key management functions such as planning, leading, organizing, and executing greatly propel the modern business industries today. All these managerial functions require the command of excellent communication skills and methods.

Take planning for example. All great accomplishments start with a detailed and intelligent planning which requires the participation of different people from different departments in a company or people with different skills. Before planning has to be started, a manager has to collect data from these groups of people. Business communication greatly aides, both the manager and the members not only for this process but for the succeeding processes that involves communicating the plan, coordinating with the right group of people, delegating the tasks, giving instructions and monitoring the results.

Skills in Business Communication: A Priority for Employers

Excellent skills in business communication rank among the top priorities that employers seek in job hunters, studies and surveys reveal. Due to the fact that most job hunters have honed their skills through training and education to be better in their own fields, many have neglected the importance of developing and improving their communication skills. For this, those who possess excellent communication skills are more likely to land jobs especially in tight employment markets where the competition is intense and the jobs are limited. While serving as a powerful career filters that most business establishments employ, your ability to communicate will ensure your higher chances for success regardless of the economic situations.

The skills in communication, however, are not a rare talent or feat. Like any other skills, it can be learned or improved. With diligence and with the right references (including this book), you too can become as effective a communicator as the most skilled ones in the market today.

Professionalism in Business Communication
Another quality most employers look for in an applicant, in addition to his or her technical knowledge in business, is professionalism and possession of "soft skills". Soft skills refer to the set of career qualities which include the ability to work well with colleagues, communicate well and solve work-related problems, among others. These sets of skills are considered the priorities when looking for future employees.
These skills, however, are rare and many entry-level workers do not possess these skills are inexperienced to put their knowledge to good use. Here is the comparison of the difference between professionalism and unprofessionalism in business communication:

- **The way they talk.** *Unprofessional* habits in communication include ending a sentence in an unusual intonation pattern called the "uptalk" which makes a sentence sound like an interrogative one; filling the pauses with awkward words and sounds like "ahh", "uhm" and "like"; using profane and informal language; and not minding the grammatical structure of the sentence. *Professional* communication habits require that a person must sound education, compassionate, well-mannered and matured.

- **Electronic mails.** *Unprofessional* writing habits include misspelled words, incomplete sentences, senseless chatting and the use of exclamation points in every sentence. These careless and messy forms of messaging give the impression that the sender does not know the proper way to communicate. *Professional* communication habits that employers look for in an applicant include the ability to clearly distinguish between the parts of a sentence as subjects, verbs and correct punctuation marks.
- **Email addresses.** *Unprofessional* email addresses are messy and comical. Some use words to make their e-mail addresses sound cute or intimidating. *Professional* e-mail addresses should include the person's name, and positive expression that would give a desirable impression on the part of the owner.
- **Voice mails.** *Unprofessional* voice messages feature loud and distracting noise in the background or contain prank messages and weird sounds. *Professionalism* in voice communications entails that the voice mails should be valuable to the recipient. It should contain information as to where the person

sending the message can be found or how he or she can be contacted for follow-up.

- **Telephone.** When answering or making calls, *unprofessional* habits allow background noises such as loud music, movies, soap operas or any TV programs playing in the background. *Professional* attitude in business communication requires a person to put of those words to facilitate in the ease of communication and exchange of information.

- **Mobile phones.** Answering or making calls during conversation with fellow employees or during meeting, or engaging in a mobile phone call with loud voice that others can't do but hear the conversation are some of the *unprofessional* habits in mobile phone communication. *Professionalism* dictates that mobile phones should be turned off or put to silent mode when you are working, except of course, when talking on the phone is part of your job.

Modern Trends in the Business World that Makes Communication Skills Important

World of work and business has undergone numerous changes over the years. Aspects of the world of work such as the form of management you will employ, the kind of work you do, the working environment you are exposed to and the people you work with have all undergone changes. Among the many new trends and changes that require effective communication skills are:

- **Innovations in communication technology.** Advancement in communication technology has not only affected the personal, interpersonal and social lives of the many; it has also revolutionized how communication is done in the work world. Modern means of communication has enable exchange of information in the business world. These include the use of mobile phones, voice mails, fax, laptop and netbook computers, smart phones, tablets and phablets. These means of communication has enabled workers to conduct meetings around the world through wireless networking, teleconferencing, videoconferencing and satellite communications. Even social media such as Google+, Facebook, Twitter, and Instagram help people in the business to collect information and sell products and services to customers.

- **Intensified global competition.** Many American markets are transcending from domestic markets. Thus, there are times when you will be required to interact with a diverse and multi-cultural group of people where your business communication skills will prove to be very useful. You will need to learn about many cultures and develop skills such as sensitivity, patience, tolerance and flexibility.
- **Trimmed management layers.** Since flattening the hierarchies of management is a practical way of increasing competitiveness and reducing expenses, many businesses have had reduced the numbers of their managers. Thus, frontline employees are tasked to make some of the decisions and communicate them to executives, workmates and clients.

- **Flexible working arrangements.** The advent of wireless and high-speed internet has created a new working condition: more and more workers are no longer constrained to an office setting working eight hours a day. With the flexibility in the working arrangement this advanced technology offers, workers can either work at home or even on the road. In a study, telecommuting employees now comprise 11 percent of the total workforce. This number steadily increases each year. Workers in this arrangement need to coordinate with fellow workers and managers from time to time.

The Communication Process

With the above indicated trends in the modern business world, the most successful ones will be those who possess highly competent and developed skills in communication. The new business environment requires a person to communicate often with a number of people. In order to better understand business communication, let us look at the processes involved.

- **Conception of idea.** This first process is one of the most crucial as this determines most of the outcome of the communication. This is influenced by how a person feels, what point of view he or she looks from, what his or her backgrounds are, and what type of situation is that calls for the communication.
- **Encoding of the message.** This is the process where the idea is transformed into something that could convey it to others either through written

words, spoken language, physical gestures or the combination of the three. This is also a crucial stage as a communicator needs to select his or her worlds and the way he or she conveys the meaning to ensure that the recipients or audience understand it exactly the way he or she means.

- **Transferring the message through a medium.** This is the process where the message is sent to the intended audience or recipients. The following mediums of communication are most frequently used:
    - **Voice over Internet Protocol.** Most internet-based businesses and companies use VoIP more than traditional phone service. The main reason being that VoIP is a lot cheaper than the latter. Interviews are often conducted through VoIP services such as Skype. This enables a face-to-face communication between the employer and the applicant without actually meeting in one place.
    - **Multifunctional printers.** The usual communication process based on the "print and distribute" principle is gradually shifting to "distribute and print" with the advent of multifunctional printers and devices that incorporate a copier, a fax machine, a printer and a flatbed scanner into one machine.
    - **Voice recognition.** Spoken messages can now be converted to a written communication through the use of voice recognition software. With improvements on the technology,

computers are now able to transcribe as much as 160 words per minute with increasing accuracy. This greatly helps those who have heavy dictation loads, attorneys and physicians by enabling them to create documents, compose and send electronic mails, input data or even control devices through the use of their own voice.

- **Multi-media presentations.** Presentations have been greatly aided by this technology for years. The most common tool used is PowerPoint. Multi-media presentations, which use sound effects, digital photos, flash animations, and video clips, can be projected from devices such as laptop or handheld smart devices and could be shared online for future reference.
- **Tweets, FB posts, blogs, and podcasts.** Many tech-savvies are already benefitting from these innovations the Internet has brought us. Tweets and FB are among the most popular ways companies are using to communicate with their customers. Most companies nowadays realize that social media is among the most visited sites in the internet by people of all ages, and background. To gain more visits in their websites, the create Facebook pages and twitter accounts which they use to posts updates with links to their website or blog site. Another way companies communicate with their clients is through blogs and podcasts.

Unlike conventional websites, blogs (blog sites) are websites with journal entries where others could post comment on the entries. Businesses usually use blogs to post information sons customers and employees and to receive feedback. A podcast, on the other hand, are audio and video files which could be downloaded to computer or handheld smart devices for listening or viewing.

- **Web conferencing.** With the improvements in technologies that utilizes the Internet, people can now share conferencing events even if they are of different and remote locations. Web conferencing offers exchange of text-based messages, and video and voice chat which could be done simultaneously. Other uses of web conferencing are training events, lectures, presentations and meetings.
- **Voice conferencing.** Conference calling technology allows a group of people to share the same call from any location. Contrary to typical voice call where only two parties could talk to each other, in voice conference calls, two or more people could exchange messages through voice. Communicators at each end could hear what each party hear what each party says. There are devices that also enable each end of a phone call to be shared by more than one person thus expanding the possibilities with voice conferencing.

- o **Videoconferencing.** Telecommunication technologies allow people to conduct video conferences or the simultaneous exchange of video and audio transmission. Unlike the typical videophone call where two people could converse while seeing each other's face on the screen, videoconferencing allows more people to conduct conversations or conferences while seeing the faces and hearing the voices of every party in the videoconference. The advent of faster computers and internet connections as well as improvements in the quality of cameras has allowed a group of 2 to as many as 200 people to hold conferences even in remote areas.
- **Decoding the message received.** This is one of the crucial part that determines the success of the communication. If the recipient or the receiver understands the message exactly the way the sender wants him or her to, then the communication is a success. The difficulty to convey the message as exactly as the sender wants to is usually difficult for written communication. Message decoding in the part of the recipient is much easier and more efficient if the communication is done with the aid of voice or video components where the recipients decoding process is aided with the tone of the voice and the facial expression of the sender.
- **Receiving feedback from the recipient.** Feedback from the recipient allows the sender to know whether the recipient has received the message

and whether he or she understood it. Feedbacks also inform the sender whether there is missing, inaccurate or insufficient information contained in his or her communication.

Chapter II. Developing Your Listening Skills

Communication is always a two-way process. By now you must have realized that business environment and conditions do not merely require a person to be the source of communication. Often, there are times when he or she becomes its recipient or audience. Since a great deal of communication is visual and aural, excellent business communications skills involve great listening skills. Sadly, however, while most of us realize the importance of being good senders or sources of communication, some of us do not possess the right listening skills.

Barriers to Effective Listening
According to a research, the range of efficiency of a person gaining information from listening is 25 to 50%. This inefficiency in listening skills has caused companies to lose money and have affected the professional relationships of people involved in a business.
To improve the listening skills, one must first realize the hindrances to effective listening.

- **Physical barriers.** These are the physical impediments which prevent a person from listening effectively. It could involve poor sound from a microphone, bad acoustics (sound reverberates so much that it is impossible to understand the words being said), noisy surroundings and inability to hear due to disabilities. It also refers to physical ailments or conditions such as boredom, illness and fatigue which makes a person unable to focus on what is being said.

- **Mental barriers.** Preconceived notions and ideas unique to a person's experience, personal values and principles, cultural backgrounds and ethical considerations could affect how to react or behave towards the process of acquiring information from listening. These notions affect what we perceive to be right and important. If the ideas that are being presented do not agree well with these notions, often we tend to block out the speaker and fail to receive the message.
- **Language-related barriers.** The inability of the listener to understand a word or a phrase due to its unfamiliarity can render the communication process futile because they have no meaning for the receiver. No matter how attentively a receiver listens, if he or she cannot make something out of the message, then communications is a failure. There are also words that impact other people's emotions strongly. A sender must also consider using those as intense emotions could cause a listener to be distracted.
- **Speed of thought.** Boredom, which is apparent in most business communication setups like conferences and meetings, can be attributed to the fact that listeners process information thrice as fast as the speaker could say them. Being bored causes the minds

of the listener to wander off thus reducing the efficiency of the communication.
- **Non-verbal distractions.** Other distractions which could affect the way we listen to speakers are the way they look and move, awkward speech mannerisms and unusual body movements. Since humans are primary visual, these distractions could greatly reduce the efficiency of the transfer of message from the speaker to the audience.
- **Faked attention.** Probably inherent to our social skills, most of us have developed the skill to look as if listening even if not. This includes faked eye contact, nodding, and impromptu facial expressions and responses. This is one of the most serious threats to effective listening because the speaker is unable to tell that the listeners' mind is already wandering off somewhere and not paying attention.

How to Build Powerful Listening Skills

The effects of the barriers in listening can be reversed by the conscious effort to listen attentively. You can't simply allow your mind to wander off and decide which kinds of information to absorb and disregard. You have to be involved in the communication process in order to be an effective listener. The following are some of the useful steps in overcoming the hindrances to and become an effective listener.

- **Modify your surroundings.** Take away those that could distract you from listening. You can minimize the sound by turning off the sources of unimportant sounds such as TVs or media devices such as mp3 players and iPods. If the sounds from the outside contribute to the distraction, you can minimize it by closing the windows and doors. Opt for a place free from distraction.

- **Stop talking.** You can't listen and talk at the same time. By forcing your idea to others while they try their best to convey to you theirs, you limit the harmonious exchange of ideas and become an ineffective listener. Instead, allow the person to explain their views first. Actively force yourself to concentrate on what the speaker is saying rather than on your comment, reaction or idea.

- **Be open-minded.** Our personal biases, beliefs and values often cause us to be selective in the kind of information we want to take in. To improve your listening skills, train yourself to listen objectively. Realize that your personal beliefs and values may not be always true, correct or applicable in all situations. Give the speaker the same fairness you would want to be extended to you had you been the speaker. Hear what is actually being conveyed rather than look for what you want to hear.

- **Develop receptivity.** Train yourself to be positively receptive in all kinds of information. Do not go ahead of yourself by judging that the information is too much for you to handle. If the information is difficult and complex, accept it as a challenge and as an opportunity for you to expand your limits.

- **Lookout for the main points.** Looking out for the main points does not only keep you attentive, it will also help you remember what the speaker is trying to say long after the activity is over.
- **Do something on lag time.** During breaks or lag times, review the main point of the speaker. Remember and evaluate the evidences and supporting details the speaker had for each point. Don't allow your mind to wander off. Instead, make good use of your sound judgment by trying to anticipate and guess the speaker's next point.
- **Practice restraint.** Have the speaker present all his points and ideas before giving your comment or reaction. Your concept of the speakers idea may be different from that of what the speaker is trying to convey and you could jump to false assumptions and conclusions without letting him or her finish his or her whole argument.
- **Concentrate on the speaker's ideas not on his or her appearance.** Don't focus on the speaker's appearance, mannerisms or his or her manner of delivering the message. Instead of allowing yourself to be distracted by these useless factors, concentrate on the ideas of the speaker. If it will help, take notes and reword his or her main points.
- **Take notes.** It is impossible for a listener to recall with perfect accuracy everything that he or she has heard (unless you're a freak). It might help if you take notes for you to remember the points and facts later. Be selective in your note taking. Do not include everything that you hear. Doing this will not only

stress you out, put you off focus and tire you but will also keep you off the main points. Choose only the important points and jot them down in the fewest possible words without compromising their meaning. Doing this keeps your note taking from interfering with your concentration.

- **Respond.** Be responsive in order to encourage the speaker and to aid him or her in the delivery of the message. Maintain eye contact, show facial expressions and nod in agreement to the points you really agree about. On certain parts, ask questions to the speaker. Doing this greatly benefits both the speaker and the listener.

Chapter III. Non verbal Communication Skills

Effective communications skills do not only involve dealing with verbal messages. Often, it involves expressing and interpreting nonverbal expressions of information and messages. Some nonverbal cues are even more effective than spoken words in conveying the message. This includes facial expressions, eye contact, and body movements, among others.

Nonverbal communication includes both intentional and unintentional expressions through unwritten and unspoken means. These physical cues have a strong effect both on the speaker and the receiver. The process of understanding nonverbal communication is actually difficult than it sounds. One of the main problems with it is misinterpretation. An act of modesty could be mistaken for a manifestation of fatigue or disinterest; a consistent eye contact for coldness or aggression; or crossed arms for defensiveness.

Effective and skillful communicators know the importance of nonverbal message in communications. More people put faith in nonverbal messages when their meaning becomes in conflict with verbal messages. A study supports this by finding out that 9 out of 10 of the messages we receive are nonverbal.

Components of Nonverbal Communication

Experts agree that it is impossible for a person to avoid communication. Even without words, a person's behavior, facial expression and movements are capable of revealing his or her thoughts and impressions.

These are the three means a person could communicate nonverbally:

- **Facial expression.** According to experts, the human face is capable of displaying as many as 250,000 expressions. With the multitude of the ways a face of a person can look through various emotional states, it has been one of the most effective ways of conveying a message. With the exception of some who are capable of controlling the facial muscles to fake or hide their emotions, most of us display our emotions openly and are manifested through the many facial expressions. Simple expressions as a smile, clenching of the teeth, or raising or lowering of the eyebrow is capable of conveying messages without the aid of spoken words.
- **Eye contact.** The ability to sense sincerity and honesty by observing and evaluating how a person makes eye contact is an inborn lie-spotting skills we are blessed with. This always proves why some says our eyes are the windows to our soul. Eye contact could also express trust, admiration, fear, distress, and distrust. These and many others are they ways we communicate with others through our eye contact—even sending messages that we cannot effectively convey through spoken language.

- **Gestures and posture.** The posture of a person conveys many messages as much as eye contact and facial expression. It can convey confidence, reluctance or shyness. There are even some thoughts that could be expressed effectively with simple movements of the body. Pulling away the body of a person from a speaker suggests disconnection and disgust, for example, while leaning towards the speaker suggests the opposite.

External Components of Nonverbal Communication
Three external elements can also convey information in the process of communication in addition to the three stated previously. They are:
- **Time.** Our usage of time tells observers about our attitudes and personalities. For example, taking time before facing someone could convey the message of self-importance; or taking time in talking with people could convey the message of interest and respect.
- **Territory.** People tend to maintain zones or territories of comfort and privacy. How a person allows other into it could convey message of the quality of bond he or she has for with them. For example, scientists have observed the existence of four kinds of zones of comfort a person has for others depending on how close a person is with others during communication. The four zones are intimate zone (1 to 1.5 ft.), personal zone (1.5 to 4 ft.), social zone (4 to 12 ft.) and the public zone (12 ft. or more).
- **Space.** How we make use of the space also conveys messages. How we decorate, for example a space, be it

a dorm room, an office, or a bedroom, determines what kind of communication we are willing to be at with others. A formally decorated space, for example, encourages a stiffer and more impersonal conversation.

How to Build Strong Nonverbal Skills

To benefit from the use of nonverbal communication, which could greatly enhance your business communications skills, follow these:

- **Maintain eye contact.** Although this could be interpreted differently in other cultures (which by the way needs to be considered first before making this first step), in countries such as US and Canada, eye contact denotes credibility, trustworthiness, honesty, fortitude, attentiveness and interest.
- **Use movements of the body to show interest.** Nod whenever an idea that you approve of is introduced in the conversation. Look alert and smart by observing proper posture in standing and sitting.
- **Be evaluative.** Although nonverbal cues are difficult to interpret, being evaluative and observant can help decode their meanings, most of the time. When there are verbal cues that seems to confuse you or contradicts with verbal meanings, seek for additional cues by asking indirect and polite questions.
- **Improve your skills in decoding messages.** Be observant. Watch for body movements, facial expressions and eye movements. This could improve the way you communicate with others.

- **Observe yourself.** You may want to know how you send out unconscious and involuntary verbal language. Knowing how you respond nonverbally could help you deal with them better. Record a conversation or have someone record it for you. Then watch and evaluate yourself. You can ask for the help of friends or family members in evaluating your behavior. You can also ask them to monitor your movements so that you can better be equipped with ample information and suggestions in evaluating your conscious and unconscious gestures and body movements.

Chapter IV. Cultural Considerations in Business Communication

While interpreting the meaning of the verbal and nonverbal components of communication is difficult, business communications involving people of different cultural backgrounds gets way tougher.

The unique cultural heritage of a country and their national experience creates a culture with aspects that are highly different from other cultures. One of those is the interpretation of nonverbal language. While various media are successfully introducing the Western culture and values throughout the world, variations in customs and values still exist. Without considering those, one could make the mistake of misinterpretation.

Business Communication with Intercultural Audiences

Here are the effective ways on how to communicate with audiences of different cultural background, effectively:
- **Simplify your language.** Use familiar words and speak brief and concise sentences. Avoid technical terms and slang. Be cautious when using idioms as the can be difficult to understand literally.
- **Speak and enunciate every word clearly.** English is not something that everyone uses every day, so be careful with your rate of speech. Emphasize

points by pausing and stopping. Number your points for the audience to clearly distinguish them.

- **Encourage the listeners to paraphrase what you say.** Having to construct a sentence for the points they have heard is a better way of assessing comprehension than nods, smiles or the fake assurance "yes".
- **Check for comprehension.** Do not wait until the end of your speech over to verify whether the audience understood what you want to say or not. Instead, verify for comprehension by asking questions every now and then. Do not proceed unless the information presented earlier is understood.
- **Observe eye movements.** Blank stare or glaring eyes are powerful cues that the mind of your audience is wandering elsewhere.
- **Accept blame.** If a there has been problem with how the message was understood, accept the blame. After all, the responsibility of making them understand what you mean lies on you.
- **Listen attentively.** If they can't seem to finish as sentence or have difficulty finishing what they want to say, just let it be. Do not attempt to interrupt or finish their sentence for them.
- **Send follow-up letters.** After conversations, follow-up with a letter to confirm the results of the agreement. For documents such as contracts and proposals, have them written in the local language of the recipient through the help of a qualified translator.

Writing for Intercultural Audiences

In sending letters to colleagues, partners, bosses or clients with a different cultural background, consider the following points:

- **Hire a translator.** Have the documents written in the local language or dialect of the recipient especially if they are very important (legal documents) and if you want to be more convincing.
- **Be concise.** Use simple language and write as few words and sentences in as little as three paragraphs as possible without affecting the meaning of the message you want to convey. The ideal length for a sentence is 20 words and a paragraph must contain no more than 8 lines.
- **Use simple language.** Use relative pronounce to ensure clarity in your introductions. Do not use idioms or words that are not common. Avoid acronyms and abbreviations. If they are repeated throughout the letter, ensure that they are defined clearly at the beginning. Use active voice; active voice clearly presents the doer and the action without confusion.

Chapter V. Qualities of a Good Business Communication

The variety of communication tools available today and the number of ways a person can communicate with another renders an effective business communication critical in the workforce nowadays. The following are the considerations an employee must have in order to be effective communicators:

- **Simplicity.** A good communication, whether written or oral, must be simple and straightforward. The purpose of any business communication is to express, inform and persuade. Here are some guides to ensure simplicity in language:
    - **Consider your audience or recipient.** Consider their area of expertise and their knowledge. Remove words and jargons that might not be appropriate or will not be understood by the audience. The more expressed and comprehensible the language is, the better. Simplify and lower the choice of words. Look for synonyms that are more common and can easily be understood (e.g. use happened for transpired or problem for conundrum).
    - **Organize the flow of thought.** This is particularly important in instructions. The message should be presented in a way that each

sentence follows a logical and chronological order that is easy to follow and understand. Always review your communication. Outputs may differ from following the same set of instructions in different orders. A confusing and disordered communication may not get you what you want in the end.

- o **Use active voice.** Active voice is preferred over passive voice because the construct is simpler. The doer and the action are clearly indicated. Passive voice sounds more formal and detached while active voice is straightforward and clear.
- o **Use simple presentation.** Although a well decorated communication may appeal to the visual senses of the recipients, it is important to ensure that the decorations does not get in the way of the text or does not steal the attention of the reader. A good communication effectively balances out the headings, subheadings, font style, images, color and white space without distracting the reader.
- o **Use brief sentences and paragraphs.** Long sentences are like spoken chain of words that would leave a speaker breathless long before he or she finishes the sentence. Not only is it tiring and boring, long blocks of texts are also confusing and difficult to understand. With so much information stuffed into a sentence, a reader could have a hard time figuring out the

real message that is being conveyed. Instead, separate each idea into a sentence. As much as possible, limit your sentences to not more than 20 words. This way, your points are easily understood. Refrain from using long paragraphs. If possible, find a way to express what you wish to say in as little sentences as possible. If not, break long paragraphs into several paragraphs. To make your point clear, you can use subheadings to guide the reader of what to expect to read from the paragraph.

- **Accuracy.** A business may not only require the written form of communications. Often, it will need other forms of business communications such as press releases and advertisements. Although advertisements are primarily graphic in nature, without texts or spoken words the advertisement will remain ineffective. With this, accuracy in the information contained is crucial. It defines the distinction between a credible company from one that has yet to establish a name. Consider the following tips of ensuring accuracy in business communication:

    o **Verify the facts.** The most important thing to consider in any written or oral communication especially that which will be read or heard by many, is factual accuracy. Your communication may be persuasive and easily understood but without accuracy, it is as useless as nothing.

- **Check your spelling and grammar.** Nothing ruins a reputation than a failed grammar and spelling. Even small ones could cause a big difference in how a recipient sees the company or the sender. Even an error with just a single letter could make a difference in the meaning of the words being conveyed. You can use spell and grammar checkers. However, it is advisable to never rely on them. Nothing beats a thorough checking of the article when it comes to error spotting.
- **Use a reference or a guide.** References such as style guides are important tools in ensuring consistency with the document produced. There are books that contain guides for proper noun use, postal abbreviations, and commonly confused and misspelled words which could be a good guide to ensuring that the documents are as perfect and professional looking as possible.
- **Have someone else read and check it.** Another way to ensure accuracy in your communication is to have someone, an objective outsider, read or hear it. Sometimes, writers fail to detect unclear contents or errors because they know what they mean and they read with the meaning on their minds. Making someone else check it is a good way to ensure that these errors are checked and dealt with. It is important that the person who will check

your contents must be knowledgeable in proper grammar, style and punctuation.
- **Use the main idea as the lead.** Start each paragraph with the topic sentence. This way, the readers will know your point just by reading the first sentence. Do not embellish the paragraph with sentences that merely expands the topic sentence. The succeeding sentences mush focus also on supporting it. Give details that will inform the readers of the "what", "how", "where", "when and "why" of the topic sentence.

- **Completeness.** The recipients of any form of message, be it written or verbal, require that the information they read or hear is complete. Completeness in the information satisfies all the questions of the reader or listener thereby saving time on follow-ups and inquiries.

Say, a client requires technical information about a product because he wants to convey the said information to the end users. In this case, providing him or her with complete information is necessary for your client to market the product well. It would also greatly benefit him if you could provide additional information that is not known to anybody—be it positive or negative. That way, he or she can do things to deal with the issue—either to neutralize the negative or enhance the positive. A way to ensure completeness in your content is to ascertain that the five W's and one H are answered:

- **WHO?** This pertains to the person component of the information. It could be the source or the target recipient.
- **WHAT?** This pertains to the object and event component of the information. This is the body of your communication or written information.
- **WHEN?** This pertains to the timeframe or schedule component of the information. This could be the launch date of the event, schedule of a meeting or specific product information such as the expiration date of the product.
- **WHERE?** This is the location component of the information. This could be the place of the meeting or assembly, the address of a company or office or the mailing address of customers or end users.
- **WHY?** This is the reason component of the information. Recipients need to understand the objective of the "what" component of the information. Thus, it needs to be explained through this.

- **Succinctness.** Considering that most people involved in business have little time for everything, in order to be effective, verbosity in language must be avoided. Communication, be it in writing or speaking, must maintain terseness or economy by expressing

more with less words. Here are the ways to shorten your sentences without affecting the overall thought:
- **Replace vague with the right words.** Mark Twain believed that one should use the most exact words when speaking or writing when he compared the difference between the right word and the almost right word with the lightning and the lightning bug. In their desire to be impressive, often, writers express what they mean in vague, riddle-sounding group of words. Often, there are words that are equivalent to those lengthy phrases which are more powerful. These words can better express what you mean.
- **Evaluate every word in the sentence.** Although it may sound boring and tiring, but checking every word in the sentence and evaluating whether they clearly express what you mean is the only way to make sure you are using the right words. It a word or some of the words does not serve the purpose of expression and only makes the meaning vague, your can delete or replace them.
- **Combine sentences.** Another way to make your sentences or paragraphs short is to combine sentences which could be expressed in a single sentence.
- **Omit detailed information about the client.** As one of the best ways to ensure conciseness in communication is to include

only pertinent information, including detailed information about the client is a no-no.
- **Avoid unnecessary explanation.** Just state objective or the purpose of the information and stop there. You will not convince the readers or audience with too many explanations about trivial things. Focus on the necessary.
- **Avoid repetition.** Unless the purpose of the repetition is to emphasize a point, never repeat things especially trivial ones. Unnecessary repetition does not only clutter your information and mess up with its logical flow; it is downright boring, too.

- **Considerateness**. The business world is run by humans. No matter how rigid the business environment is, one must still consider the contents of his or communication and the impression the audience or reader will form for those contents. Here are the steps to ensure considerateness in business communication:
  - **Create the impression of selflessness.** Instead of using "I" or "we", consider using "you". Your audience and your readers will be more interested if they know what in it for them.
  - **Be positive.** Focus more on the positive facts. Nobody wants to be constantly reminded of failures or to be blamed.

Chapter VI. On Business Writing

There is not one aspect of a business world that does not involve writing. The credentials you used when you applied for job, the cover letter you used to impress your employer and the message you sent your family when you told them about your successes all involve writing.

Since the rise of the Internet, the importance of professional written communication has tremendously increased. The very means of communication has changed and has been expanded. Emails have enabled exchange of professional and business correspondence in a matter of seconds. The advent of online advertising and publishing has also made it simple for businesses to communicate with their customers.

Skills in business writing help a person to communicate with others effectively. With the right and effective business writing skill, a person can ensure that the letters he or she sends, along with memos and ads convey his or her message accurately. If the purpose of the communication is to give information, a person's writing skill could help convey accurate and correct information. If its purpose is to convince, a good skill in writing could make the recipients agree with a person's point. In the world of online publication and advertising, excellent writing skills is important because people tend to scan and skim online contents. Being an excellent and effective writer could spell the difference between dead contents and contents that are actually read by online visitors.

Skills in writing help save time and money.
An ineffective writing creates obscurity and confusion and it would cost a company money and additional effort to deal with the problems that may arise from this. Unclear writing could provide inaccurate and incorrect information which could either make people require for explanations, form assumptions or even start taking legal actions. An inefficient and ineffective writing could not only cost money; it could also slow down business.

On regular business days, there are instances where an employer has to send emails notifying his or her employees of a meeting or giving them instructions for a job. These written communications must be brief and easy to understand to save time. Not only does good writing adds credibility to the employer, it also boosts the image if the company.

Skills in writing have many applications
Skills in writing are important in various communications of the company such as reports, sales materials, brochures, audio-visual presentations, emails, memos and visual aids. In addition, the size of the operation of the company necessitates written form of communications through email because of the convenience of sending multiple messages to various employees or clients at once rather than having to talk to them one by one. With the right skills in writing, not only will the recipients understand the contents of the letter,

it will also effectively convince the recipients of the contents of the letter.

Excellent writing skills are also necessary when it comes to attraction, selecting and hiring the most appropriate employees. Human resources managers need to possess the necessary writing skills in order to appeal to applicants who have the right qualifications and job experience. Good writing skills also save a company money as placing advertisements and hiring copy-writers costs money.

What You Need To Know About Written Communication In Business

Just as heading somewhere without a concept of a destination or a map to guide your journey is useless and senseless, so is preparing for a business communication without an idea of what to do. Surprisingly, business writing differs from other forms of writing that you may have done in the past.

When you were younger, you were required to write compositions and term papers for school in which the primary purpose is for you to discuss your opinion or emotion and to express what you know about the topic. This is because your teachers and instructors wanted to assess your learning and thought processes. In business, writing a letter or the text for the oral and visual presentation follows the following guidelines:

- **It must be purposeful.** Your writing must be guided by an objective. Furthermore, its primary purpose is to present the problem and the corresponding solutions. It must be informative, and the solutions outlined must be effective and well thought of.

- **It must be convincing.** The point being presented in the message, whether it is an opinion or a course of action that you, your team or your company is advancing, must be presented in such a way that your audience accepts and believes them.
- **It should be brief.** It must be direct to the point, and the main points must be well emphasized.
- **It must be audience oriented.** It must be prepared using the perspective of the user instead of yours.

These guidelines do not only make writing easier; it also ensures that your audience effectively understands what you prepare. The skill in writing for business communication that follows the above-stated guidelines is not acquired easily. Very few people, those who are born with the knack for it, are capable of writing effectively without training. Following a systematic process, however, makes the task and the process of learning a lot easier.

The Writing Process for Better Presentations and Messages

The tasks that require writing skills specifically tailored for business include e-mails, memo, letter and oral presentation. Following a systematic plan in preparing those is a practical way of ensuring that the business communication achieves its primary purpose. The process of writing includes prewriting, writing and revising.

- **Prewriting.** Writing requires preparation. You do not just proceed to writing right away. Twenty-five percent of the writing process involves the preparation done before the actual writing.

    o **Evaluating and identifying your objective.** Before composing a message, ask yourself these questions:
    - *Why are you sending the message?*
    - *What do you want to achieve with the message?*

    o **Selecting Your Communication Channel.** After evaluating your purpose, the next step is to select the best way to deliver the message. Some message achieves greater impact when sent as a hard copy instead of an e-mail, some if delivered orally and some could just simply be sent through SMS. The following must be considered in choosing the best channel for communication:
    - Significance and urgency of the message
    - The type of feedback required
    - The time required for the feedback to be received
    - Necessity of a permanent copy

- Cost of communication for the said channel
- Degree of formality
- Confidentiality of the message
- Sensitivity of the message

One of the concepts that helps guide the selection of the right channel for communication is the theory called *media richness*. This theory states that the medium or channel of communication determines how a message is represented. Furthermore, the theory states that the channel of communication recreates the actual message. The following are the channels most often used for communication and the guide on when to select them:

- **E-mail.** Use e-mail when there is not much urgency in acquiring feedback. This form of communication though has security issues, which could compromise the privacy of the communication.
- **Blog.** Use this when presenting information through the Internet to make the information available to the public or to a group of people.
- **Face-to-face conversation.** This is a rich form of interactive communication medium. Use this when presenting bad

news and personal messages. Furthermore, use this form of communication if you want to be more persuasive.
- **Face-to-face group conversation or meeting.** This is another rich form of an interactive communication medium. Use this when the opinion and decision of the group are important for the task. This should not be done if the sole purpose of the communication is information dissemination as there are communication mediums which are more efficiently suited for that.
- **Instant Messaging.** This is useful if you want to get a quick response. This is most useful for fast answers and for service-related chats with customers.
- **Letter.** Use this form of a communication medium when formality or a written record is necessary.
- **Phone call.** Use this as an alternative to meeting in person when nonverbal cues are not necessary, and you need to gather or send information quickly.
- **Text Messaging.** Unlike chats where there is an exchange of messages in real time, text messages are sometimes not read or responded to as fast. Use this to leave short messages without having to call.

- **Voice-mail message.** This is important for leaving important messages that the recipient can respond to at his most convenient time.
- **Wiki.** This is useful for making information available to others. This is also useful for information where collaboration or group participation is required as participants can easily add, remove or modify contents.
- **Video or audio conferencing.** This is useful for instances where the group needs to pool in their opinions and arrive at a decision but cannot arrange a face-to-face group meeting because of geographical dispersion of members.
- **Memo.** This written record clearly outlines policies and procedures and collects information within the company or organization.
- **Fax.** This is useful for sending in written records, especially when the message is required to cross international boundaries or when it is important to send a message quickly.

o **Anticipating the recipient of the message.** A good communicator anticipates the personality of the recipient or audience of the message and bases his or her message through the concepts he or she forms of the recipient. You are more likely to attain your communication goals if you create a profile the recipient/s of your message.

- **Profile your recipient.** Visualize your audience or recipients. This way you can tailor the contents of your communication, specifically to the personality of the readers or listeners. An oral presentation before a group would require more audience anticipation compared to a letter to a colleague or a regular client. In addition, remember that the recipient/s of your communication will always look for the information that would give them a benefit.
- **Respond to the profile.** The form of the message contained in your communication is greatly shaped by the profile you make of your audience. Factors such as language choice and level of formality very much depend on what the receiver would find positive or negative. Another factor that you would want to consider when forming your message is the secondary audience. Your primary audience or recipient, sometimes, will forward your message, as is, to another with or without your

knowledge. Realizing the possibility of your message being forwarded to someone, and anticipating your secondary audience, will help you shape the message to suit both your audiences.

- **Modifying the communication to suit the task and the recipient.** An important aspect of a message that must be modified in order to suit the recipient is the tone. The tone, which is determined by the choice of words in the message, affects how the recipient feels upon hearing or reading the message. A number of adaptive techniques enable a skilled writer or communicator to transform the message into something that imbibes a positive tone.

  - **Emphasize the benefits of the audience.** One must make into his or her guideline the words of Ben Franklin when writing for a business communication. He said that to be good, a communication ought to have a tendency to benefit the reader. A communication that puts emphasis on the benefits of the reader is a powerful one.
  - **Use second person instead of first person.** Messages that are focused on and concentrates on the benefits of the

audience naturally contains the second-person pronouns *you* and *your* instead of the first-person pronouns *I, we, us* and *our*. It has been observed that the second-person pronouns catch the attention of the reader better than the first-person pronouns.

- **Developing the right writing techniques.** Unlike conventional writing where the main objective is to be expressive as much as possible, writing for a business communication needs to be effective and persuasive in order to benefit the organization or company. Below are the three ways to improve the readability and effectiveness of the communication:

  - **Be conversational while maintaining professionalism.** Communications sent through e-mails, letters, memos and reports offer a chance to be conversational instead of being overly stiff or formal. It must be remembered, however, that a writer should avoid being too casual or being too formal in writing the communication. This is because being too casual gives off the wrong message that the letter is unprofessional and low-level. To maintain professionalism while being conversational, a communication must sound matured and educated. Expressions such as *BTW* for *by the way* and other similar acronyms, over usage of words such as *like* and *you know*, and using emoticons or smileys give the impression that the message is of juvenile origin.

- **Be positive in your expressions.** Positive language improves the tone and clarity of the communication better than negative language. A positive communication focuses on the solutions, advantages, and gains rather than on the problems, disadvantages and losses.
- **Be polite.** Being polite in your communication involves the avoidance of rude language as well as words that are nagging and demanding. One effective way of softening the tone of the communication is to convert the imperative from a command to a request with the word *please* and supporting it with details and reasons.
- **Avoid biased language.** Be cautious when using the words that might be biased. Be sensitive with issues such as gender, ethnicity, age, race and disability. As much as possible, avoid including the words *his or her* in the message. Avoid specifying the age or

using words that are demeaning based on age.

- **Writing.** Nobody is excluded from the experience of writing a message. Present day business conditions, with the advent of modern communication technology, necessitate the frequent exchange of messages. The quicker you can come up with the ideas and the better and more efficient you can express and explain them are positively correlated with your fulfillment, happiness and success in your career. The writing process outlined below will make it writing a lot easier and faster.

    - **Research and gathering of information.** Accuracy is one of the most important attributes of a good business communication. To ensure this, a research is necessary before writing the communication. The collection of information and data before writing is guided by what the receiver needs to know, what he or she needs to do, how and when should it be done and the consequences of his or her inaction. Research is necessary, especially if the information required is beyond your experience or knowledge. There are two kinds of research methods:

        - **Formal.** Lengthy and detailed reports as well as complicated solutions to complex business problems usually require this form of research method. The following steps are involved in the formal research method:

- **Manual search.** This involves looking for relevant data or information through resources found in libraries. The traditional sources of information include magazines, journal articles, books, handbooks, dictionaries, directories, almanacs, reference books and newspapers.
- **Electronic search.** With the rapid growth of the Internet, many web resources have been established. Some universities and libraries have even established online resource pages. Most books nowadays have electronic versions, too, which could be accessed via the Internet. Electronic search involves data gathering using those resources. Furthermore, resources such as CD's, DVD's and databases provide additional information, although those sources are either rarely found

nowadays or their contents are accessible through the Internet.
- **Surveys and interviews.** Much of the information, however, specially updated ones that are client-related, can be accessed by going directly to the sources of the information. This can be done by conducting surveys, interviews and by distributing questionnaires either manually or electronically.
- **Experiments.** Although this form of research is timely, this is one of the most reliable. Conducting experiments will provide you with accurate and up-to-date information that are verifiable.

- **Informal.** Collection of data and information for regular and common tasks such as memos, reports, presentations and e-mails can be done through informal research methods such as:
    - **Accessing the files.** Often, simple inquiries can be answered by accessing the company files or by consulting the appropriate person or workmate.

- **Direct inquiry.** If your boss requires you to make a communication, the best way to get the information is to ask him or her.
- **Informal survey.** Informal surveys through phones or questionnaires could also prove useful in data and information gathering.
- **Brainstorming.** Although a brilliant mind is enough to arrive at ideas, a pool of minds can make the task enjoyable, simpler and sometimes better.

o **Organizing the information.** After gathering the necessary and relevant data and information, the next step is organizing them. Having the ideas grouped and organized help the readers understand what the communication is trying to convey. Unorganized ideas, on the other hand, give the impression of sporadicity and aimlessness. One of the best ways to organize your ideas and information is through outlining.

o **Writing the message.** Effective and persuasive messages contain varied sentence patterns and avoid common sentence errors.

They achieve parallelism as well as emphasis through various techniques in writing.

- **Use the four sentence types.** When writing, it is best to mix various sentence types such as simple sentence, compound sentence, complex sentence and compound-complex sentence rather than repeating the same sentence pattern.

- **Control the length of each sentence.** Regardless of what type you use, sentence length is one of the greatest influential factors in achieving readability and clarity that affect comprehension. It is best to limit sentences to 20 words or less. A study reveals that comprehension is inversely dependent on the length of the sentence. Sentences with eight words, for example, were found to result in a 100% comprehension rate while 19 to 20 words result in an 80% comprehension rate.

- **Avoid common sentence errors.** These errors in business communication are proven to reduce the credibility of the writer:

- **Fragments.** Most fragments, or incomplete sentences, are the results of errors in punctuation. Sometimes, independent clauses are separated unintentionally from dependent clauses because of the usage of a period rather than a comma.
- **Run-on Sentences.** This occurs when two independent clauses are run together either without a punctuation (usually semicolon (;)) or a conjunction (*or, nor, but, and*).
- **Comma-splice Sentences.** Independent clauses that are joined by a comma result in a comma splice. These sentences must be joined by a conjunction or separated by a semicolon instead of a comma.

- **Emphasize.** Emphasis in oral communication is done by varying the tone and amplitude of the voice while expressing the main idea or by repeating them slowly. Hand gestures, facial expressions and creating auxiliary sounds (e.g. by pounding the desk or table) are effective tools, too. The following are ways to achieve emphasis in print:

- **Emphasis through mechanics.** Mechanical emphasis in writing is achieved through underlining, using italics or boldface, changing the font, using all caps, using dashes and tabulating.
- **Emphasis through style.** One of the most effective ways of emphasizing a point is with words and sentence constructs to emphasize the main idea and to de-emphasize unimportant or negative ideas. This is achieved using vivid words, placing the main idea on the first sentence, and placing important ideas in a simple sentence.
- **Achieve parallelism.** This is done by balancing the parts of the sentence. Sentences that observe parallelism are easy to read and comprehend.

Revising. The last and the most crucial step in business writing is the process of revision. In here, you ensure that your communication achieve its purpose while becoming grammatically flawless. Revision should be done with the purpose of achieving clarity, conciseness, directness and vigor. Revision also includes designing or modifying the design of the document to achieve readability and visual appeal.

Conclusion

There is no perfect time to hone your communication skills than now. With the accelerated rate at which the working conditions are changing where companies are delegating more managerial tasks such as decision making and accomplishment reporting to ordinary employees, an application can increase his or her chances of employability by enhancing his or her communication skills.

Like most other human skills, while the knack for communicating effectively, both in written and in spoken forms, is determined by genetics, it can be learned and honed through constant practice.

The information and tips detailed in this book cover most of the communication aspects in the business world. Included here are guides and instructions on how to improve your writing skills and polish your speaking skills in terms of form, content and way of delivery.

The next step is to continue to practice. Learning, as most experts believe, is a continuous process. You are never fully learned. Given enough time, effort and patience, you will become one of the most effective and efficient communicators in the business world.

www.ingramcontent.com/pod-product-compliance
Lightning Source LLC
Chambersburg PA
CBHW071812170526
45167CB00003B/1282